We Read
PHONICS™

A Day at the Zoo

TREASURE BAY

Parent's Introduction

Welcome to **We Read Phonics**! This series is designed to help you assist your child in reading. Each book includes a story, as well as some simple word games to play with your child. The games focus on the phonics skills and sight words your child will use in reading the story.

Here are some recommendations for using this book with your child:

1 Word Play

There are word games both before and after the story. Make these games fun and playful. If your child becomes bored or frustrated, play a different game or take a break.

Many of the games require printed materials (for example, sight word cards). You can print free game materials from your computer by going online to www.WeReadPhonics.com and clicking on the Game Materials link for this title. However, game materials can also be easily made with paper and a marker—and making them with your child can be a great learning activity.

② Read the Story

After some word play, read the story aloud to your child—or read the story together, by reading aloud at the same time or by taking turns. As you and your child read, move your finger under the words.

Next, have your child read the entire story to you while you follow along with your finger under the words. If there is some difficulty with a word, either help your child to sound it out or wait about five seconds and then say the word.

③ Discuss and Read Again

After reading the story, talk about it with your child. Ask questions like, "What happened in the story?" and "What was the best part?" It will be helpful for your child to read this story to you several times. Another great way for your child to practice is by reading the book to a younger sibling, a pet, or even a stuffed animal!

I'm thinking of an animal that starts with the letter "s."

Is it a seal?

LEVEL 7

Level 7 introduces words with vowel combinations "ou" and "ow" (as in *out* and *owl*), "oi" and "oy" (as in *oil* and *boy*), "aw" (as in *hawk*), "oo" (as in *book*), and "oo" (as in *cool*).

A Day at the Zoo

A We Read Phonics™ Book
Level 7

Text Copyright © 2012 Treasure Bay, Inc.
Illustrations Copyright © 2012 Meredith Johnson

Reading Consultants: Bruce Johnson, M.Ed., and Dorothy Taguchi, Ph.D.

We Read Phonics™ is a trademark of Treasure Bay, Inc.

Published by
Treasure Bay, Inc.
P.O. Box 119
Novato, CA 94948 USA

Printed in Malaysia

Library of Congress Catalog Card Number: 2011942419

Hardcover ISBN: 978-1-60115-349-4
Paperback ISBN: 978-1-60115-350-0
PDF E-Book ISBN: 978-1-60115-595-5

We Read Phonics™
Patent Pending

Visit us online at:
www.TreasureBayBooks.com

PR-6-12

A Day at the Zoo

By Bruce Johnson

With illustrations by Meredith Johnson

Help prepare your child to read the story by previewing pictures and words.

1. Turn to page 4. Point to and say the word *outside*. Ask your child to describe what she sees in the picture. Point to and say the word *zoo*. Ask your child to describe what someone might see at the zoo.

2. On page 5, point to and say the word *booklet.* Ask your child to describe what might be written in the booklet.

3. Turn to page 6. Point to the picture. Ask your child to say the name of the animal in the picture and to describe the animal and the habitat. Ask your child to point to the word *hippo* on the same page.

4. Continue "walking" through the story, asking questions about the pictures or the words. Encourage your child to talk about the pictures and words you point out.

5. As you move through the story, you can also help your child read some of the new or more difficult words.

Phonics Game

Word Families

This game will help your child read words that appear in this story, as well as words that have the same ending.

Materials:

Option 1— Fast and Easy: To print free game materials from your computer, go online to www.WeReadPhonics.com, then go to this book title and click on the link to "View & Print: Game Materials."

Option 2—Make Your Own: You'll need paper or cardboard; pencil, crayon or marker; and scissors. Make 6 cards that measure 2 x 4 inches. Print these word family endings on the cards: out, ound, ook, ood, ool, oon, oil, and oy. Make 14 smaller letter cards that measure 2 x 2 inches. Print these letters on the cards: p, t, sh, b, f, h, m, r, s, c, l, st, w, n.

1 Place the larger word family cards face down in one pile. Place the smaller letter cards face down in a draw pile.

2 The players all take three word family cards and place the cards face up in front of them. The first player then draws a card from the draw pile and tries to make a word using one of his endings. If a word can be made, the player places the card in front of the word ending. If a word cannot be made, the card is placed in a discard pile.

3 Play continues. Players can take a card from the draw pile or the discard pile. Players can make multiple words with each word family card, simply placing new letter cards on top of others.

4 Play ends when the draw pile is empty. The player who creates the most words wins. Mix the cards and play again!

The sun is out and it is hot. It is a fine day
to be outside. What can you do? You can
spend a day at the zoo!

Grab a booklet as you go in. It will tell you what to look for. You can start out with the big animals.

Look at the cute, brown baby hippo!
Its mom is called a cow. Mom
and baby stay cool in the pool.

Do not miss a visit to the big cats. Big cats make lots of sounds. You may hear a growl or a loud roar!

This panda bear is eating bamboo shoots. It grips the bamboo with its paws and peels it. Bamboo is the food it likes the best.

 Chimps are the clowns of
the zoo. They enjoy howling
and goofing around.

This zoo has a house just for birds.
The roof is very high to give them room
to fly.

Inside this house you can see a
hoot owl. Or a wood duck.
Or a pretty cockatoo.

This hawk is on the lookout.
What do you think it sees?

The zoo has an insect house. Some insects hide in the soil. Some can hide on a leaf. Can you see it?

The reptile house has critters that
crawl and coil and creep. Some kids
like this house best of all!

Some reptiles like to stay
wet. They can be found in
the reptile pool.

This zoo has animals from the sea too. This is a manatee. It is also called a sea cow.

Look at the seals! Seals
like to play in the pool. Some
seals can play a horn. Toot, toot!

Toot!
Toot!

Outside it is hot. In here it is chilly. These animals like to stay cool.

Look at this girl petting the sheep. It is okay to pet animals in this part of the zoo. You can give them food too.

Put in a coin and the food spills out. Now feed the animals that you like best.

You may see zookeepers around the zoo. They are there to take care of the animals.

21

Zookeepers feed the animals. They
clean the dens, houses, and nests. They
clean the animals too!

A zoo vet has a big job. He must keep the animals well. He checks ears and looks inside of mouths.

The zoo is a fun place to see all sorts
of animals. You will find out many things
about them too.

The next time you want to spend
a day outside, visit the zoo.
You will really enjoy it!

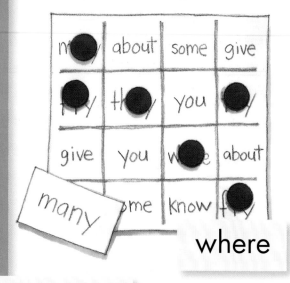

Word Bingo

Play this game to practice sight words used in the story.

Materials:

Option 1—Fast and Easy: To print free game materials from your computer, go online to www.WeReadPhonics.com, then go to this book title and click on the link to "View & Print: Game Materials."

Option 2—Make Your Own: You'll need nine 3 x 5 inch cards; paper or cardboard; pencils, crayons, or markers; ruler; and scissors. Write each word listed on the right on a 3 x 5 inch card. Then create some Bingo cards with your child. Each player can make his own card. Start by making a 4 by 4 or 5 by 5 grid. Fill the grid with random words from the list. Words can be used more than once. (See example illustration above.) Create some colored dots to put over the words.

1 Mix the word cards and place them face down. A player turns over a card and reads the word.

2 Players put a dot on the words on their Bingo card if matched. If the word appears more than once on a card, put a dot on each one.

3 The first player to complete a row, across, up and down, or diagonally, wins the game. Then, play again!

where

you

some

many

they

fly

about

know

give

> I am thinking of the word *outside*. What are the sounds in the word?

> "ou," "t," "s," "i," and "d."

I Am Thinking

This is a fun way to practice breaking words into parts, which helps children learn to read new words.

1 Explain to your child that the word *mouth* has the sounds "m," "ou," and "th."

2 Ask your child to say all the sounds in the word *loud*. Answer: "l," "ou," and "d."

3 When your child is successful, say: "I am thinking of the word *outside*. What are the sounds in the word?" Correct answer: "ou," (as in *out*) "t," "s," "i," (long *i* as in *side*) and "d."

4 Repeat with the following words. Start with the prompt: "I am thinking of the word. . . . What are the sounds in the word?"

Suggested words:
brown, clowns, lookout, bamboo, shoots, hoot, booklet, hawk, paws, enjoy, coin

If you liked *A Day at the Zoo*,
here is another **We Read Phonics** book you are sure to enjoy!

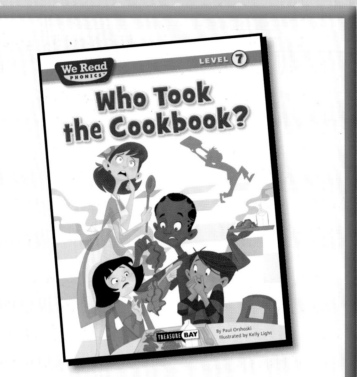

Who Took the Cookbook?

The cook in the lunchroom serves great food! But now her cookbook is missing and her cooking and food are just awful. Where is the cookbook? Did a crook steal it? Join the hunt to find out who took the cookbook!